# Friction Free
# Sales and Marketing

Three Types Of Psychological Resistance -
Which Stop Your Customers From Buying?

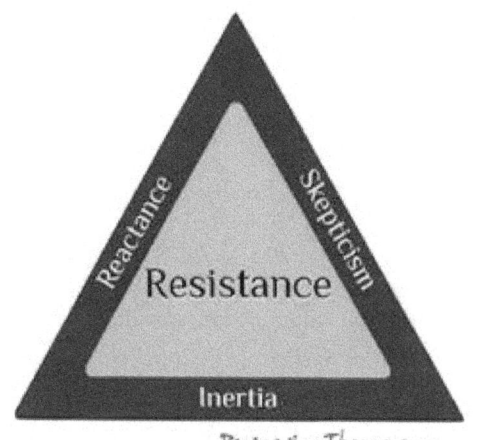

## By Matt Fox

Subscribe for more at:
**PersuasionTheory.com**

# DEDICATION

To my bride, Kathy.
Thank you for this fun life together.

# CONTENTS

Section 2: Skepticism

Section 3: Inertia

# INTRODUCTION

Congratulations on taking the first step to making your customer's buying process much easier. After you've gone through this book, you'll realize why you stop yourself from buying something you originally wanted to buy. You'll also notice stopping points keeping your *potential* customers from becoming paying customers. And, hopefully you'll convert them into lifelong raving fans.

This is a workbook, not just an eBook. There are small exercises to help you gain the most benefit from this book. Take time to do these. You don't have to do all the exercises but, like everything in life, the more focused practice you put into this the better the results.

A little background before you dive in.

## How The Brain Works

I'm not going to go into details on your brain's chemical reactions and how the various parts of the brain interact with each other to create resistance. Even though these details are important, they are better left for academics to discuss.

You want results, not theory and scientific notes. This workbook is designed to give you those results. If you want resources to look into and learn about this, send me an email.

Just realize there are many neurological processes and psychological issues behind what we do as humans. To sum it up, **our brains are wired to seek pleasure and avoid pain.**

## Traditional Training

Most traditional training teaches you to pitch the features and benefits of what you're selling. When I first got into sales, I was told to discover the buyer's "hot buttons" and keep pushing them. We wanted to go on and on listing each of the benefits and how it helped hit the buyer's "hot button."

I was taught to create long bullet lists of benefit statements and benefit driven headlines on my sales letters. Everything was about the many fabulous things the customer was going to receive after buying our products. Keep stacking on the benefits!

We were taught to overcome objections, but that wasn't dealing with the resistance a customer felt during the buying process. That was about handling the reactions the customer voiced during the sales pitch, or in his head while reading a sales letter. It wasn't about taking a few simple steps to prevent the objections from popping up in the first place.

That's what this workbook is about.

## This Isn't New

If you've seen any new sales & marketing trainers, or read any of the many new books on behavioral psychology & economics, you've probably seen the results of many of these ideas and techniques.

What's been happening over the years is a scientific realization about the many things top salespeople and top direct response marketers have known unconsciously for years. Academics are finally learning how to test these theories and codify the results in ways to make it something that's teachable.

You've seen some, if not most, of these techniques before. Each won't apply in every situation. But they're important to understand because each person you talk with, and each market you target, will react differently.

This workbook gives you the tools you need in your toolbox. You'll be able to pull them out and use them properly when you need them. Or, if you are unsure, this will help you test and find out which tool will work best.

At the least, you'll have a new way of thinking and approaching the influence process and interacting with everyone you meet.

## About Manipulation

Please don't send me complaints about how this can be used to manipulate people. That would be very manipulative of you. Because a gun, a pill, or a knife can kill someone does not make it a bad thing. The intention you hold while using these tools makes them do bad things. If you do not trust yourself, stop now. If you're comfortable you can use these with responsibility to make the world better, please continue.

Also, you use these techniques whether you're aware of it or not. I recommend you read through this and make sure you're using all the techniques in the most ethical and responsible manner.

Go make the world a better place for you and everyone in your life.

Enjoy and have fun,
Matt Fox
PersuasionTheory.com

# RESISTANCE PROTECTS YOUR CUSTOMER

We are motivated by two factors: achieving pleasure and avoiding pain.

When you think about what you want for dinner tonight you want to eat something delicious (seeking pleasure). If you're watching your weight, you hope you can also eat something that's healthy (pleasure of treating yourself well while avoiding the pain of gaining weight) so you can lose weight (avoid the pain of stepping on the scale and experiencing shock) and fit into those jeans you bought several years ago (seek pleasure of accomplishing goal, improving health, appearance, etc.).

As you can see, there are many factors that go into any decision you make. Most of this is unconscious and happens faster than you can blink your eye. Each piece of the decision will have more weight on the result you choose depending on your core values. When you're doing things that meet your core values you'll feel pleasure (happy, joy, proud, etc). If you're not meeting your values you'll feel emotional pain (upset, anger, frustration, etc.).

That's where resistance comes into play. When you're resistant there's something tugging at you because of a fear

1

of pain. There's something unanswered or stopping you. You don't know if something will pop up and smack you in the face if you take a step forward.

## Resistance is a protection mechanism.

When I had my insurance agencies, we occasionally would present home and car insurance premiums drastically less expensive than what the customer was currently paying. Even though we could be saving them a lot of money, thousands of dollars sometimes, they would hesitate. Why?

They start asking questions like:

- Is this just some introductory price?

- Does XYZ insurance company pay their claims; will it be difficult if something happens?

- Who do I call if I have a billing problem?

- Are they going to cancel me after we start the policy?

Most people aren't familiar with insurance. They have a bad taste of the industry long before we ever started talking. They didn't have any problems with their prior insurance company before calling us. The fear of changing to something worse started to creep in. The fear of the unknown.

Most of us are comfortable. Your life is fine right now (I hope). So why change?

There are many great things that could happen.

There are many bad things that could happen.

And that's where resistance protects you.

## This Is About Creating Change

This is about making changes in a person's behavior. Yes, like most people reading this, you want to use it to get people to buy something from you or opt-in to your list. You want some type of business result from this workbook, which is great.

When you're helping someone buy your product, you're creating change. You're changing a behavior, a decision, a belief, an attitude, something so they'll move from "non-buyer" to "buyer."

Because this is about changing behaviors, you can use these to help make changes with your children, spouse, significant other, friends, coworkers, etc. Or, you can use it to change a behavior in your own life.

It's about more than business. You simply have to think of the possibilities.

Even though it's bigger than sales or marketing, keep your work focused on one topic when going through the worksheets. You'll benefit most when you apply your practice to a narrow topic. Remember, light focused into a laser beam can cut through steel. Focus your energy into one area of your life or business. You can always come back and work on other areas when you're ready.

# THE THREE TYPES OF
# PSYCHOLOGICAL RESISTANCE

I divided this workbook into three sections (not including the Introduction and Conclusion). One section is devoted to each type of resistance. This categorization comes from the work of Dr. Eric Knowles and his book *Resistance and Persuasion*[1].

I don't know if Dr. Knowles was the first to classify resistance into these three categories. It is how I've come to categorize and identify resistance when working to make change in others.

The three types of resistance are:

1. **Reactance** (The Reactive) - Resistance to the **sales process**. Your customer feels like he's being pushed. The sales process and techniques you're using are causing the resistance.

2. **Skepticism** (The Skeptic) - Resistance against

---

[1] Knowles, E.A., & Linn, J.A. (2004). *Resistance and Persuasion*. New Jersey: Lawrence Erlbaum Associates, Inc.

your **offer**. Your customer doubts if your offer is the best thing available to him.

3. **Inertia** (The Lump) - Resistance to **change**. This is resistance in the buyer and has nothing to do with you, the process, or the offer. Your customer is happy (or not miserable) where they're at and not in any hurry to change.

Each type of resistance can appear in your customer at one point or another. Because each have a different cause, there will be certain points where one type of resistance is more likely to appear and easier to head off. Keep this in mind as you're working with your customer.

I may also call a customer a "Reactive" or "Skeptic" or "The Lump." I am not saying a person will only exhibit that type of resistance. When I call someone a "Lump" I mean he is displaying a particular type of resistance, inertia. He is demonstrating a resistant behavior at that time **only**. He is not always resistant to change (the definition of Inertia), only at that point in the sales process is the resistance showing and at other times may show skeptical or reactive forms of resistance

Each person is different and any individual can be different at different times.

Got it?

Good.

# OVERVIEW WORKSHEET

In this worksheet I want you to get a general idea of resistance you've experienced. Once you begin to understand what it's like for you then you'll be better identifying and preventing it from arising in others.

1. Think about a time when you experienced Reactance (resistance because of someone's sales process). Write down what it was like and how you reacted.

_____

_____

_____

2. Think about a time when you experienced Skepticism (resistance to/skepticism of a sales offer). Write down what it was like and how you reacted.

_____

_____

_____

3. Think about a time when you experienced Inertia (resistance because you didn't want to change). Write down what it was like and how you reacted.

_____

_____

_____

4. What ways resistance has helped you or harmed you?

_____

_____

_____

Register to download printable copies of all the worksheets mentioned in this book at http://persuasiontheory.com/u/ffsm-book

# SECTION 1:
# WORKING WITH THE REACTIVE

Have you ever bought a car from a car dealership? Stop groaning. I know negotiating with a car salesman is about as much fun as rolling naked on broken glass. In fact, you may prefer rolling naked across broken glass over dealing with car salespeople. Why is this?

## Pressure

Buying a car isn't fun for multiple reasons. The reason most people hate buying a car is the uncomfortable pressure the salespeople put on you throughout the negotiation **process**. You're like little kids trying to push over a giant sumo wrestler but the sumo keeps rolling over you until you cry "uncle."

**You experience Reactance when you feel like you're being pushed into buying. It's a reaction evolved from the *sales process*.**

When you begin applying pressure or requiring commitments from your customer, they begin to pull away. Something inside causes him to jerk away, disagree, raise objections, or stop reading your sales letter.

It stems from the fight or flight response. You've cornered your customer into making decisions and he will either come out swinging or run like hell.

This form of resistance can also develop at the beginning of the sales process.

For example, I have a strong reaction when I know I'm going to speak with a salesperson. I don't like to answer questions beyond "yes" or "no." I hold back. I know what a salesperson is looking for. I know their "tricks." I don't want to be baited and sold. I want to buy. And when I start to hear "sales speak," I'm immediately triggered to go into a negative state. This is another form of Reactance.

In marketing, it's a little more difficult to know what's going to trigger the Reactive unless you know your niche. If you do any marketing online, you've probably seen people complaining about "long sales pages with the yellow highlighter and screaming headlines." These letters work for many markets but there are many others that don't like this type of sales letter and it elicits the Reactive resistance.

Reactance can also develop out of a long upsell/downsell process. If you've ever bought a domain or web hosting through GoDaddy.com you'll know what I mean. After you click "buy now" for the domain you want, up pops a page of add-ons for you to buy. Whether you choose some add-ons or not, after you click next, there's another page of offers to buy. It seems to go on forever (and a reason I don't use GoDaddy). It's obviously working for them but they've lost many people, like me, because of their horrible process.

So how do you eliminate this reactance in your buyer?

# THE REACTIVE - OVERVIEW WORKSHEET

Write 3 examples of times you've experienced reactance to a sales person?

_____

_____

_____

What triggered the responses?

_____

_____

_____

When have you noticed your customers reacting to your **sales process**?

_____

_____

_____

Register to download printable copies of all the worksheets mentioned in this book at http://persuasiontheory.com/u/ffsm-book

# CREATE A RELATIONSHIP, NOT A ONE-TIME SALE

Nobody wants to feel like another notch on the headboard of your sales career. You don't want to wake up the next morning knowing you were used for someone else's gain. (If you do, go on to the next tip. This isn't for you.)

Yes, it's important to watch your sales numbers and pay attention to your conversion rates, cost per lead, etc. However, when working with your list, niche, tribe, or whatever you want to call your prospect base, emphasize your relationship with them. Make them understand this isn't a quick sale for you, even if it's the only thing you sell. You want to be a friend, a consultant, an advisor, a helper, etc., not another drooling salesman.

It is funny to me how, over the last few years, social media is buzzing with how they're changing the sales process. Many there say, "You're finally able to build a relationship with your customer base."

I disagree.

Good marketing is always about building a relationship. We did it with direct mail and newsletters years ago (and in my businesses last year). Letting your customer know you're here and plan to be around to help out in the future goes a long way. Social media is simply another way to extend the relationship experience.

Blogging is becoming a way a small business can build relationships. It helps you establish your credibility and knowledge. A blog is more than a single page website with sales information (also known as a glorified brochure). A blog allows you to provide value before **and** after the sale. Your goal is to become an advisor in the eyes of the customer, not a salesman only out to empty their wallet.

*War! huh-yeah*
*What is it good for?*
*Absolutely nothing*
*Say it again y'all*
- From the song "War" by Edwin Star

The US military is doing what it can to change the relationship with terrorist cells overseas. They have teams whose goal is to help those immediately affected by the terror groups understand we're not their enemy. They're walking around in military garb extending their hands. They help build schools, take care of kids, and build better lives for everyone so we can all be better.

You can change the title on your business card from "Product Salesman" to "Consultant" if you want. But, if your goal is to go in and carpet bomb the customer with your high pressure sales techniques and make the sale despite the relationship, you'll continue to fight each and every day of your career. When you become a consultant, ask the right questions, and build relationships that go beyond the sale, you'll end up with a raving fan who will help you over the long run.

# MAKE IT A RELATIONSHIP - WORKSHEET

Marketing: How can you emphasize the relationship you'll have beyond the sale? What are you doing to demonstrate a relationship before the sale (newsletters, emails, etc?)

_____

_____

_____

Sales: What questions can you ask to become a trusted friend/consultant/advisor instead of a sales person trying to close a sale?

_____

_____

_____

How can you make the customer feel like the "expert" in your area so they're making the decision and not being "sold?" How can you change the relationship from you influencing him into the customer influencing you he needs your product?

_____

_____

_____

Register to download printable copies of all the worksheets mentioned in this book at http://persuasiontheory.com/u/ffsm-book

# IT IS NOT ABOUT YOUR CUSTOMER

Sometimes I think the customer is sitting there listening to the little devil and angel sitting on each shoulder. One side is the devil encouraging the resistance. On the other shoulder is the angel telling him all the great reasons to move ahead. Sometimes we say, or do, something that makes the devil start screaming like a five year old, "Why do *I* have to do that!?!?"

## It's Company Policy

What he doesn't realize is your request is not about him (as a person). When you have requests that may raise resistance, tell them it's "company policy" they have to do this. Your request is not about the customer; it's your standard operating procedure to fill out a 5 page intake form. It's your standard contract everyone needs to complete before you can move ahead, etc.

Making a decision or action part of your "company policy," your customer won't internalize it as something only he has to do. It becomes a hurdle everyone has to jump and avoids the "Why do *I* have to do that?" resistance.

You get the idea?

## Tell A Story

Ahhh, stories. Those elegant fables that take you traveling on magic carpets to exotic lands where glittery pixies hula dance to loud reggae music. Or not.

However... Stories remove the resistance from your customer. Stories place him as the character in your story where you can overcome the reactance with ease.

Stories (metaphors) have been used for thousands of years to pass along friction free teachings. A story causes you to **turn off the critical part of your brain**. You become immersed in the flow of the characters and allow the message to easily sink in...free from resistance.

Think about the last time you watched a movie and you found yourself having an emotional reaction. Maybe you started to tear up, or you felt the stress or panic in the character. Stories force us to put ourselves in the character's shoes so we can relate to what's happening.

Stories don't have to be long drawn out tales. You can easily create a story by saying, "I had a customer like you once, and this is what happened with him/her..." Then, continue your story and match the situation to what your buyer is experiencing.

You can use a story to weave through any problem or objection. Show him how the previous customer moved past his concerns with your solution. Your customer will begin relating the issues to himself. And he'll begin the process of finding solutions for himself.

It really is that easy.

In fact, when I told a friend of mine about storytelling he gave it a try. He was nervous. He hesitated at first. He was afraid he would do it wrong. But, he decided to use it with the next person he had to deal with.

He told me how anxious he was at first. He thought the customer would see through his story as some trick. As he got into it, he said his customer sat there listening intently and ended up buying. His customer told him the reasons he bought were the exact same reasons my friend shared in the story. He couldn't believe how easy it was.

Are you paying attention now? Did you realize I just used the story principle in the last paragraphs?

If you don't have another customer to use in a story you can talk about yourself. Remember talking about yourself is generally a bad idea. You never want to brag about how wonderful you truly are. However, you can easily tell a story that makes you a hero, demonstrates your intelligence, shows how you solved this problem, or whatever. It's your life story, you find the solution. (If you want a great book on stories to tell, get *The Story Factor* by Annette Simmons – Find links to all resources mentioned in this book at http://persuasiontheory.com/u/ffsm-book.)

## It's Just Like...

Last, the second easiest way to create a persuasive story is with the "it's just like" strategy. Using this strategy, you can easily create quick, off the cuff stories with layers of meaning by adding "it's just like..." to the end of your sentence. Then, follow-up with what it is like and how it will eliminate his resistance.

If this seems a little confusing that's because **it's just like** riding a bike. When you first started, it was challenging to stay balanced while pedaling. You didn't think you would ever figure it out. But you did. Now, after all these years, you can jump on any bike and start riding with ease. And this will become natural too. You just have to jump on and start riding.

I have an article about the "It's Just Like..." technique on my site. You can find the link to this article and all other resources mentioned in this book here: http://persuasiontheory.com/u/ffsm-book.

# IT'S NOT ABOUT YOUR CUSTOMER - WORKSHEET

Review the steps in you sales process. What could be mistook as a personal situation?

_____

_____

_____

What steps can you change and make it "not about your customer?"

_____

_____

_____

What stories can you tell? Write down some examples of other customers overcoming common objection points:

_____

_____

_____

What's *your* story where you personally solved a similar problem?

_____

_____

_____

What do you think storytelling is like? (The "it's just like…" strategy.) Practice this with everything over the next week.

_____

_____

_____

Register to download printable copies of all the worksheets mentioned in this book at http://persuasiontheory.com/u/ffsm-book

# BRING IT DOWN TO SIZE (MINIMIZE THE REQUEST)

If I ask you to help me move over this upcoming weekend you'll probably say, "I'd love to help but I'm busy that weekend helping my mother-in-law raise a barn with her Amish support group."

However, if I ask you to help out for only a couple of hours on Saturday you may think it's not a big deal and end up staying the entire day (because it's fun, not because I convinced you. It's always your idea.).

Obviously, **big requests create more resistance than smaller requests**. Whether your request is for your prospect to buy your product or to opt-in to your email list, you want to make the request seem like a minimal commitment on his part.

In research by Cialdini & Schroeder[2], volunteers went door-to-door asking for donations to charity. When they

---

[2] Cialdini, R. B., & Schroeder, D. (1976). Increasing compliance by legitimizing paltry contributions: When even a penny helps. Journal of Personality and Social Psychology, 34, 599–604.

added the words "even a penny will help" to the end of the request, there were 21% more households that donated. Not bad. What makes this even better? The amount of the average donation was almost the same in both options. That's huge.

They received a 21% increase in the number of households who donated. **And the same amount of money was given from each household!**

Amazing.

## My Pay-Per-Click Advertising Experience

When I was running my last insurance agency, I used pay-per-click marketing to generate a large portion of our leads. The typical quote form on most insurance websites is several pages long. You fill out some information and click to the next page and fill out more. It feels like there's no end in sight. (There really isn't. I think they ask you to hook up an I.V. and input blood at some point.)

I didn't like that process.

Our quote forms were one page. We still required all the same information; it was just on one page and not five (or more). It required a lot of personal information. We need things like names, address, birth dates, vehicle information, etc. for everyone on the policy. In our tests, one ad with the words, "Fill out our fast, 1 page quote form" outperformed others drastically.

Even though we still required almost the same amount of information, we made the request seem simple and short. We told them it was a "fast, 1 page quote form." (Also, the form itself reduced friction because the visitor could see all the information required on the form and could easily determine how fast they could fill it out.)

## Demonstrate A Minimized Request

If you do any online lead generation you'll find you generate more leads when you require less information. So, if you want only the visitors name and email address, remove all unnecessary information requests on your opt-in forms. Lose the fields requiring your prospect's phone number, address, business title, etc. You'll get many more leads with less information. It reduces the fear of annoying phone calls (or stalkers standing outside your home) after filling out the form.

However, test this for results. (Do I say that a lot? If you said "no" you'll change your mind by the end of this book. Test everything.)

If a small form gets you 1000 leads, and the long form only gets 100 leads but these 100 leads produced 10 times more in sales, you'll want to use the longer form. Ultimately, this is always about the bottom line. Keep that in mind.

## How about another example?

Let's say you have a product with two price and feature options. Your "Basic Package" is the lower priced product and gives all the features *most* buyers need. Your "Complete Package" has premium pricing and gives your customer all the features plus a bunch of extra stuff beyond the Basic Package.

One way to test the *Minimize The Request* method is to write copy similar to the following near the purchase options on your sales page:

"If you were hesitant about how much this will help you, even the Basic Package will help you achieve (fill in your benefit statements)."

This is language you want to test seriously instead of using as is. As much as I'd like to say, "This improves copy every time," all markets are different. So, test this.

Whatever you do, you want to emphasize how easy, fast, small, little, quick, minimal, etc. the action is that you want your customer to take. And having someone buy your basic package is better than someone not buying anything.

# BRING IT DOWN TO SIZE - WORKSHEET

Identify all the steps in your sales process where you require a commitment or some sort of action for your customer to take. They can be the sale, making an appointment to meet, filling out a form, whatever. List them here:

_____

_____

_____

Take each step and brainstorm ways you can make the request seem smaller. How can you make it seem easier?

_____

_____

_____

Register to download printable copies of all the worksheets mentioned in this book at http://persuasiontheory.com/u/ffsm-book

# BE AGREEABLE

This method is easier to use in verbal, rather than written, persuasion. But I'll show you a nice twist you can use for writing copy.

You won't always *completely* agree with your customer, and you don't have to. However, you don't want them to think you disagree. He believes what he is saying (that's why he said it, duh?) and the easiest way to change his belief is to agree with him and then present your ideas.

What am I getting at? Check this out.

When you reply to your customer's question, here are three replies you want to keep in mind:

1. Answering "No" creates resistance.

2. "Yes, but" says you agree, but not fully and you still want to push your ideas.

3. "Yes, and..." demonstrates you're listening and you agree with your customer even if what you say after the "and" is the complete opposite.

Notice how you can make the problem worse by using the first two? It's not that it will ruin a sales presentation altogether (yet, it may) but it can create additional friction at that moment. You're probably doing this every day and don't even realize it.

Instead, when your customer objects or raises a challenge reply with, "Yes, and this will be a good choice because…" and lay out your reasons. He'll be a lot less willing to argue with you, if at all. Why?

You're not arguing with him.

If you're agreeing you can't be arguing. You're simply taking his comment and continuing on with it. Essentially you're reframing what he said in an agreeable manner. "And" is a powerful little word in influence.

Give it a shot.

Over the next few days, with your friends or family say, "Yes, and…" when you reply. Tell me how this changes your interactions. You're probably in a habit of saying "no, but…" and will have to work to break it. Once you do, email me and let me know how it changed things.

Here are other alternatives that will help you be more agreeable:

- That's right, and…
- Of course, and…
- Absolutely, and…
- I agree, and… (This is obvious to be agreeable, isn't it?)
- Good point, and…

Use it and see how far you can go by saying the exact opposite of what they said. I've had people say things like, "This is really expensive." And, I reply with, "That's right and it's really the least expensive solution you can find…" They just nod as I continue and they snap out of their trance.

## Using "Yes, And…" in writing…

If you're using this in writing, here's a quick lesson from Ericksonian hypnosis. (This works even more powerfully in speaking but is a way to incorporate "Yes and…" in writing.)

Ericksonian hypnosis is conversational hypnosis. Milton Erickson pioneered these concepts and it's where it got its name. One key way he found to get people to go into trance is to "pace and lead" with his words and body.

Pacing is saying/writing something that is true or common knowledge. If I were hypnotizing you, pacing statements would be things like, "you're sitting here" "you hear my voice" "you're thinking." These are things that are all true. When you hear them a part of your mind says, "Yes."

Leading is saying what you want your customer to do or believe. Again, more examples from hypnosis, "You're beginning to relax" "You'll make the changes necessary" "Follow my suggestions."

Do you notice the difference between the two? Basically, one is stating what's true (pacing) and the other is making stuff up (leading). Everything you say or write falls into one of these two categories (either a pace or a lead). And, when you follow this structure below you're feeding your reader the, "Yes, and…" statement. They'll be thinking "yes, yes, yes, and…" inside their head.

Here's the structure:

You start with 3 pacing statements and then a leading statement. Like this (blatantly boring example).

Pace, pace, pace, lead...

You're reading these words (pace), there are a lot of ideas available to you (pace), there's something here you want to learn (pace), and the things you learn will make a big impact in your life (lead).

Then, two pacing statements and then a leading statement.

Pace, pace, lead...

As you use what you're learning (pace), you'll come up with other ideas (pace), which will help you make better use of these tactics (lead).

Then, one pacing statement and a lead.

Pace, lead...

These tactics aren't known by most of society (pace), so you can use them wherever you want without fear of being caught (lead).

Then you randomly can use pacing or leading statements throughout the rest of your copy.

The point is to build up gradually to statements and behaviors the reader may not fully accept as true. In traditional sales, this would be a version of building a "yes" set. The theory is: If you get someone thinking, or saying, "yes" they're more likely to continue thinking, or saying, "yes" when you ask for the order.

After you've finished reading this, go read classic sales letters or listen to political & religious leaders speak (search YouTube). Try to find where they go from pacing to leading. You'll notice how they blur the lines between fact and making stuff up as they're speaking/writing.

This structure takes some practice. It will also cause you to write more. This means, in essence, it will help you build your skills even more.

## Tell People What You Want Them To Do

Stop telling people what you don't want them to do. Don't tell them "don't think XYZ" or "you shouldn't XYZ." (Yeah, I know I just said what not to do but I did it for a reason!) Tell them what you want them to do instead.

I think of my kids as the best example for this. I occasionally have to tell them to stop hitting each other. So, instead of "don't hit your sister!" I have to tell my son to "go in the other room and leave her alone for a while!" Not that my kids fight a lot. They're angels. Really.

If you say "Don't think about the cost of this project," you're causing the cost to sit in the mind of your customer. They can't **not** think about it when you bring it up. Tell them what you want them to think about. This could be the benefits they'll receive, the time they'll save, etc. Focus on the things that help them want to buy what you're selling.

Get it?

Redirect your customer's attention to what you want the customer to do. Because we can only hold a certain amount of information in our attention at any one time, make it count.

# BE AGREEABLE - WORKSHEET

Write a dozen sentences where you answer the opposite of what a customer says and alternate these at the beginning as your reply:

That's right, and…
Of course, and…
Absolutely, and…
I agree, and…
Good point, and…

_____

_____

_____

List what you want to people to do. Instead of "don't touch, please" you would write, "keep your hands to yourself, please."

_____

_____

_____

Register to download printable copies of all the worksheets mentioned in this book at http://persuasiontheory.com/u/ffsm-book

# MAKE THEM RESIST THEIR
# RESISTANCE

When people complain, they often just want to be heard. Don't get me wrong, it's not that their complaint isn't valid. Usually, it's a simple psychological need to let it out. We want to be acknowledged and validated. This method allows you to address the resistance and validate what's going on in your customer's mind before he even knows it's there.

A good sales letter will always bring up objections and address them. What are the reasons against your customer buying your product? What thought would be gnawing away in the back of your customer's mind? Find those and tackle them one at a time.

For example, if you were selling a coaching package, you can address any resistance by stating, "Some people may not want an entire 12 month coaching program because they fear the commitment. That's okay. (This is a version of 'Yes and...' as you just read) The people who invest in this coaching package go for it because..."

Not everyone will use this technique in their copy because they don't understand how powerful it can be.

That's okay. Those who do use it will find it's something worth testing and see where it helps increase conversion.

Did you see how I used it in the last paragraph?

## Why would you want to use this?

A couple of studies done by Dr. Eric Knowles[3] demonstrate the importance of this tactic. In one study research students asked unknown students walking into the common area, "Would you mail this letter for me?" The letters were stamped and only needed to be dropped into the mailbox inside the common area. 71% agreed to mail the letter. When the students acknowledged the resistance and asked, "I know you might not want to, but would you mail this letter for me?" the compliance rate shot up to 100%.

Now, these numbers may seem magical. 100% compliance would be wonderful. Wouldn't it? You could control the world with that. Who am I kidding? I'd be happy to control my kids cleaning behaviors. Anyhow, take the 100% compliance with a grain of salt.

Even though the students were walking into the common area where a mailbox was located, they had some resistance to helping out. Only 71% agreed originally. The acknowledgment of the resistance numbed the reaction. What I think happened is it creates a "yeah, they understand me," type of response and, because of that connection, any resistance dropped away.

It's obviously easier to slide this in during a face-to-face sales situation but can work just as well in a sales letter, if you know your market. Pay attention and test what works.

---

[3] Knowles, E.A., & Linn, J.A. (2004). *Resistance and Persuasion*. New Jersey: Lawrence Erlbaum Associates, Inc.

# MAKE THEM RESIST THEIR RESISTANCE - WORKSHEET

Where are the points of friction in your sales process?

_____

_____

_____

Where would it be worthwhile to test resisting the resistance?
"I know you may not want to but (your desired action)."
Or,
"I know you may not fully agree with this but (what you want them to agree on)."

_____

_____

_____

Register to download printable copies of all the worksheets mentioned in this book at http://persuasiontheory.com/u/ffsm-book

## "REVERSE PSYCHOLOGY"

The previous technique, *Make them Resist the Resistance*, is a form of Reverse Psychology.

You first used this, or were victim of it, when you were a child. Basically, you're telling someone to do the opposite of what you really want him to do.

When my oldest daughter was in preschool, she told me about some kids she wanted to play with. The kids wouldn't play the games she wanted to play. She was sad. I got on my knee and gave her kind, fatherly advice. I told her when she wanted to play with them to say, "Hey, I have a great game to play! But…um, well…never mind, you wouldn't want to play this fun game…" and then start to walk away. (I emphasized she had to stutter and stammer through the last part for best effect.)

The next day, when I picked her up, I asked how the day went. She was beaming because she got several kids to do things she wanted to do. (Proud daddy!)

My bride does this with me all the time on difficult decisions (because I have the mentality of a preschool kid). It drives me nuts because I know what she's doing. She prefaces her requests with, "I know you won't want to…"

and asks me to go to the opera or do some other horrible thing.

Even though I know what she's doing, because of the form of the request, I have to listen to make sure I don't have a knee jerk reaction.

You get the point?

Now, remember to use **this with care. It is best used with the customer who consistently disagrees with most of your suggestions.**

## Playfully Use It To Introduce Thoughts

Another way you can use this is to introduce thoughts. If I were to say, "don't think of purple kittens," you can't not understand the statement without thinking about purple kittens. Now, that's an absurd example but, when you make it playful, you can use the same thing in a sales, marketing, or personal interaction.

When I was single, I would joke with ladies about how they shouldn't think about how much fun our next few dates would be. Well, think about that. You can't imagine the next few dates without also thinking about the dates that occur before those. Yes, it is devious. Yes, it was helpful.

You can do the same thing. Of course, you wouldn't want to think about how you'll use this over the next few days. We'll get to that in the worksheets. Okay?

Now, if your customer isn't resistant to the idea, using this could backfire and actually create resistance. I'm sure you've been in a situation where this backfired. I'm not going to go into it much more. Use with care. Remember to be playful to soften the impact if you're not sure how your customer will react.

# "REVERSE PSYCHOLOGY" - WORKBOOK

Be aware and use Reverse Psychology with care. It can create resistance.

What are some steps in your sales process you want your customer thinking about?

_____

_____

_____

List the points in your sales letter, sales presentation, etc. where you can seed ideas with "Don't think about XYZ right now."

_____

_____

_____

Register to download printable copies of all the worksheets mentioned in this book at http://persuasiontheory.com/u/ffsm-book

# FOCUS THE RESISTANCE

Have you ever taken a magnifying glass in the sun and focused the sunlight to a point on the ground (or your sister's arm)? What happens? All the collected energy comes to that point and produces light and heat that can start a fire (or burn flesh that leaves emotional scars you have to hear about forever, but that's another story). You're taking all the random light waves and focusing them where you want so it can do something useful.

You can do the same thing with your customer's resistance. And, this is one of my favorite techniques! EVER!

People want to resist at some point. If you've been through any traditional sales training you may have heard, "People love buying but they don't want to be sold." When your customer objects, or has some reaction, it helps him feel like he's buying and making the decision instead of being sold.

We all have a need to resist at some level. Instead of waiting for the customer to tell you his objections, tell him what he should be reacting against. Sounds complicated, right?

If you're on social media sites, like Twitter or Google+, you may have seen this from certain social media personalities. It's a great way to build expertise and following without creating resistance.

The social media gurus use it (accidentally) by pointing out what everyone is doing wrong. They'll post something like:

- If you +1 your own post on Google+, you're doing it wrong.
- If you're using direct mail lists to build leads, you're doing it wrong.
- People who use pop-ups on their blog aren't serving their reader well.

While this somewhat implies a solution, all they're doing is pointing out where you should be angry, annoyed, resistant. Then, when you run across this situation you can say inside, "yeah, social media guru was right, that's annoying." He gets to look like the good (smart) guy. And because these become true, other things he posts slips by without you questioning his validity or expertise.

Pretty fancy, right?

You may recognize it as version of the good cop/bad cop you see on TV and movies. You're giving your customer a bad guy to rally against so he will "confess" or trust you, the good guy.

If you don't have an industry to push people against, like the social media "experts," you can point to small flaws in your product or service to resist against. You can point out the shipping time will be be longer than usual. Point out how that's a problem because your customer wants to get this as soon as possible. It, in a way, distracts from other, less important, issues and gives the person a place to focus their emotion.

You can also make other salespeople the bad guys. "You're lucky to be reading this because other persuasion 'experts' would be telling you how their product will get you to convince anyone, anytime, anywhere. You and I both know that's not true." Tell your customer how another salesperson in your office may not be so forthcoming with information related to your customer's concerns.

The point is to build up something, a real or imaginary person, a place, a thing, a group, an industry, so your customer can focus his resistant energy on that. When you tell them who, what, where, or when to be resistant it won't surprise you later.

# FOCUS THE RESISTANCE - WORKSHEET

List **things** you can direct your customer's attention on to be resistant.

_____

_____

_____

**Who** can you add to the list to direct the customer's attention at?

_____

_____

_____

**When** and **where** should your customer be resistant? List locations and/or time frames before, after, and during your sales process your customer should experience some hesitation.

_____

_____

_____

If you listed competitors, how are you being careful not to attack the competition so you keep your image in a positive light?

_____

_____

_____

Register to download printable copies of all the worksheets mentioned in this book at http://persuasiontheory.com/u/ffsm-book

# WORKING WITH THE REACTIVE - SUMMARY

Here's a quick summary of the techniques for working with the Reactive.

- Create A Relationship, Not A One-Time Sale
- It Is Not About Your Customer
- Bring It Down To Size (Minimize The Request)
- Be Agreeable
- Make Them Resist Their Resistance
- "Reverse Psychology"
- Focus The Resistance

# SECTION 2:
# WORKING WITH THE SKEPTIC

Skepticism is the type of resistance you're most familiar with. Traditional sales and marketing training teaches you to ramp up the benefits to overcome skepticism in your product. They also teach some of the ways to address it. Some of the techniques here may seem very familiar.

Don't discount these just because you've heard before. Realize these techniques work best with a specific type of resistance, skepticism. When you understand what type of resistance your customer experiences you'll make sure you hit the right areas at the right time. And you'll be able to serve your customer better.

## What is Skepticism?

**Skepticism is resistance against your *offer or proposal.*** It rises from the features and benefits of what you're selling.

Your customer is wondering, skeptically:

- Will this work for me?
- Are you honest?

- Is this the best solution for me?

Most sales training claims your buyer is skeptical because you haven't built up enough value. They tell you to crank up the benefits so you overwhelm the customer with what he'll get. You consume the hesitant buyer and push him through his skepticism. While this is somewhat true, the resistance is still there and **you risk buyer's remorse or excessive returns** on your sales.

By cranking up the benefits and not addressing the skeptical mind you're bullying your way to a sale. If you have someone who's afraid of spiders it will be difficult to get them to walk through a room of spiders, even for $10,000. You can amp up the benefits, maybe increasing it to $50,000 and a lifetime supply of spray-tan (if spray-tan is important to him), after he walks through. If that's not enough you'll have to keep building up the offer and push him through the door to go. Even if he walks through, he'll still be afraid of spiders at the other side.

By working with these principles to address the skepticism, you won't have to add on any additional benefits. You can keep your spray tanning supply and your extra money. **You won't have to throw in anything that costs you more.**

Yes, you can sell more without adding more to your offer (extra expenses). Doesn't that sound beautiful?

How do you know skepticism is popping up? And how can you keep it from continuing to pop up after you beat it down, like the whack-a-mole game?

If you're selling in person, your customer will start asking multiple questions about the details or arguing about why your product won't work. Don't argue back.

Think about all the times you've been in this situation, has arguing back ever resolved anything? Of course not.

Think about those times. That's the skepticism poking its head out and sticking its little mole tongue out at you. Use these six methods to whack the skeptical mole back down, make it tame, and walk it on a leash around the park. (You'll be the only one with a pet mole, isn't that grand?)

# WORKING WITH THE SKEPTIC - WORKSHEET

List what things a buyer would be skeptical about in your sales letter or presentation.

_____

_____

_____

What places do your customers have the most questions about your offer?

_____

_____

_____

What types of objections you commonly receive?

_____

_____

_____

Register to download printable copies of all the worksheets mentioned in this book at http://persuasiontheory.com/u/ffsm-book

# I GUARANTEE IT!

You've seen guarantees before.

They come in various shapes and sizes. There are 30-day, 90-day, 1 year, and lifetime money back guarantees. You can have a low price guarantee and/or match competitors. You can have a low price guarantee where you beat competitors advertised prices by 10%. You can have a free trial guarantee where the customer won't be charged for 30 days unless they like your product.

**Guarantees are the easiest and fastest way to eliminate Skepticism.** If you're not offering a guarantee, I can guarantee (Yes, I know) you are losing money. Consumers want some sort of security behind their purchase.

It's why they put up with touchy pat downs and invasive full body scans at the airport TSA checkpoints. It helps you feel secure another terrorist isn't going to find a way to get onto a plane.

Nothing seems to be stable anymore. Your customer wants a business he can trust; a company, a website, a salesperson, a consultant who will stand behind his product or service 100%.

If you're a small, less known, business a guarantee is even more important. Everyone knows how easily Wal-Mart will allow you to return your defective back massager, or the broken guitar you just bought for Guitar Hero. There's also a guaranteed quality expected when purchasing from a known brand like Starbucks.

If you're new to a market put up a big sign so *EVERY* customer knows you stand behind your products.

## Hyundai

Hyundai made a huge impact in the auto market because of their 10 year/100,000 mile warranty. No other car in that price range, or other price range at the time, offered a warranty like that. Why did this work?

Hyundai eliminated doubt about the quality of their cars. Their cars were reasonably priced. The guarantee allowed you to concentrate on the benefits of the Hyundai line without the nagging worry of future repairs.

What if you sell online?

I think it's even more important to make your guarantee easily visible. You have no credibility, no history, and no store for an angry customer to burn down if they lose control. It's critical for you to give and honor a strong guarantee. You also want to make it known you can be easily contacted if someone wants to use your guarantee.

## What type of guarantee can you give?

This depends on the type of business you operate.

The most obvious is the "Money back" guarantee. You

could use a 30, 60, or 90-day money back guarantees. But, if you're bold, I recommend testing a one year, or lifetime money back guarantee. You may be surprised to find your conversion rates increase significantly while your return rate slightly increases, if at all.

In my insurance agency we couldn't give a true money back guarantee. Instead, we created a "4 Point Guarantee" and gave a written copy to each prospective customer. It read:

1. Money Back Guarantee – You can get a refund of any unearned premium when you cancel your policy.

2. Privacy Guarantee – We won't sell your name or share it with anyone.

3. No Pressure, No Hassle Guarantee – We make buying insurance easy!

4. Total Client Satisfaction Guarantee – You have my commitment to your satisfaction.

As you can see, it's really nothing special. Any insurance agency can promise these things. However, like Claude Hopkins discussed when writing the Schlitz beer ads in the early 1900s, this may be the same process every other company is using, we're the only one telling the customer how we do it and that's what made us different (From his book *Scientific Advertising and My Life In Advertising*).

Be creative. You'll be surprised how a small change in your guarantee can make a big impact.

# I GUARANTEE IT - WORKSHEET

List the guarantees you can use to increase the security your customer feels when they buy your product?

_____

_____

_____

What are some best options from the list above?

_____

_____

_____

If you can offer a money back guarantee, what is the time frame now? And can you test for longer time frames?

_____

_____

_____

Register to download printable copies of all the worksheets mentioned in this book at http://persuasiontheory.com/u/ffsm-book

# THE ART OF THE REFRAME

When I was 19, I had a job framing pictures. People would bring in their prints, photos, paintings, kid's baby shirt, and want it framed to hang on their wall. That's what I did. I would help them pick out the frame and matting to bring out the best in whatever it was they wanted framed. Then, I would assemble the frame, the matting and the "art" to bring out a beautiful piece suitable for hanging on their wall.

At the time, a friend had a small scorpion problem in her home. Her father would collect the scorpions in a jar of something (I think it was alcohol but I don't remember) and throw out the jar when it was full. I asked her if I could have the jar, instead of them throwing it out, and I took the scorpions to work.

I decided to attach the scorpions to a black background, create a nice little box frame with black matting, and frame the scorpions for my friends. They were still ugly, nasty looking, golden-brown, bark scorpions, but with the black background and silver frame they looked nice; something suitable for hanging on a wall, if you're into that sort of thing.

Reframing for influence is the same thing. You're taking an idea and making it more appealing by changing the outer appearance.

The blunt description is to tell your customer X doesn't equal Y, as they thought. X equals Z instead. And Z can either be something bad for them or something good. Either way it's what you want them to believe so they decide the way you want.

Reframing is an art. There are many, many ways to reframe ideas, beliefs, values, decisions, etc. Here are two ways you can reframe to work with the skeptic.

## Reframe the Offer

The context of an offer can be as important as the offer itself. If the offer you're presenting in doesn't fit right and can cause skepticism.

In the book *Switch*[4] the authors, Chip and Dan Heath, discuss how a couple of researchers in West Virginia influenced people to eat healthier, more specifically, consume less saturated fat. They identified whole milk as the specific target. Whole milk is the largest source of saturated fat in an American's diet. The goal was to get people to drink 1% or skim milk instead of whole milk.

Instead of pitching a traditional message saying whole milk is fatty, they reframed what drinking a glass of whole milk means in fat content. Their marketing showed how drinking one glass of whole milk has the same amount of saturated fat as eating five pieces of bacon. Basically, they reframed the context from a cold, creamy, delicious drink to drinking the unhealthy grizzle from a frying pan. Not

[4] Heath, C., & Heath, D. (2010). *Switch: How to Change Things When Change Is Hard*. New York: Crown Publishing Group.

yummy and it worked.

If the milk industry is reading this, you may be able to sell more milk by changing the label from 1% and skim milk to 99% fat-free and 100% fat free milk and targeting more health conscious consumers. And it is another simple way to reframe.

In my insurance agency, we changed the idea of switching insurance companies. We told the customers they were getting a new protection team who's always on their side. We wanted to reframe it into joining a new family, not losing the old familiar agent.

When you think about what your offer is, how can you reframe it from an expense to an investment?

## Reframe the Resistance

To state this simply: Instead of letting the skepticism stop your customer, use the resistance as their reason to buy.

Have you ever had a situation when the person you're influencing starts asking multiple questions? You can sense a bit of resistance on their part. When this happens, say something like, "These are some great questions. You're obviously considering this decision very seriously. These are the type of questions that allow you to become completely comfortable with your decision to buy today. So, what else do you want to ask before you start (buy now, etc)?"

This flips the questions upside down. Instead of becoming stopping points the questions become reasons he wants to start. It may seem like a simple play on words, but it does much more. It begins creating an unconscious link in your customer's mind where more questions asked means more reasons to buy.

If you're using it in copy in a sales letter, and you know there may be resistance, tell your reader to be skeptical. Write out, "I want you to feel a bit skeptical as you read this. There's a lot here you'll want to approach with an open mind. And, as you continue reading, you'll get to the end and feel confident you're making the right decision to buy now."

Simple, no?

It's okay to be skeptical about how this will work. Spend some time thinking about it. Test it wherever you can. After you've used reframing a few times you'll see how it works and find easier and smoother ways to use it regularly.

# THE ART OF THE REFRAME - WORKSHEET

List your offer and benefits:

_____

_____

_____

Reframe each benefit to what it means for your customer:

_____

_____

_____

Go through where you've listed places in your sales process that may create resistance. List the ways you can reframe those into reasons to buy today:

_____

_____

_____

Register to download printable copies of all the worksheets mentioned in this book at http://persuasiontheory.com/u/ffsm-book

# TAKE YOUR CUSTOMER BACK TO THE FUTURE

Again, I'm asking you to help me move. I have to move everything and wondered if you would help me move **tomorrow**?

If you're like most people, you would mumble something about how your aunt has plans to take you butterfly hunting with members of her Aging Butterfly Society group. Or you would come up with some other excuse.

On the other hand, what if I asked you to help me move in three months, after we sell our home? Most likely it will have less resistance.

The outcome is the same. The time of the decision and action performed change. I moved your decision into a time in the future instead of a decision today.

Skepticism is something that occurs now, in the present. You don't want to take a risk NOW. You don't want to choose NOW. You don't want to commit yourself NOW.

People, in general, think more positively about the future.

In the future things are rosy and shiny. Unicorns dance happily along rainbows while chocolate covered fairies fart pixie stick candies that fulfill your daily nutrition need. Life is good.

**Move the decision into the future and your buyer will feel less skepticism now.**

A decision about the future, while it's being made now, actually feels more optimistic and hopeful because of an internal time shift. It disassociates you from the pain and stresses of a decision today and into a more optimistic and positive state.

This isn't putting off a sale.

This is changing the perception of time in your customer's mind.

You've probably seen this in a retail environment. This is (was) a common practice many major retailers use a couple of times each year. They offer you "No payment for 90 days" or "Interest free financing for 12 months."

You don't have the money today but in 90 days you might. Now you're a little less resistant and maybe you'll make that purchase with their 90-day credit agreement. Or you don't have enough money now, but you can easily make payments over the next 12 months and avoid their hefty interest fees. Right?

These have you moving your purchase decision out into the future 90 days or 12 months down the road, even though you're buying something today.

What if you don't have the authority to create these types of finance agreements?

You can change it up a bit. It requires a little creativity with your language, but it works.

Ask your customer, "If you were to imagine what it's like 12 months from now, after deciding to start (buy, invest, etc.) today, how good does it feel to know you made the right decision today?"

Okay, I loaded that question with a few twists in the language, but it gets him imagining the enjoyment of what it's like to own your product over the last 12 months.

This creates a time distortion effect. He's floating into the future in his imagination. While there, he's feeling how good it is to have already made the decision and is now looking back at how good the decision was to have made...today.

It's okay to reread that last paragraph to understand what's going on.

That may not overcome a "no money" objection, but it moves your customer past their skepticism today so he can imagine what it's like to be the proud owner of what you're selling. If he has other concerns he will bring those up too. Now you have something to work with.

Now, what if you were to imagine a year out and looked back to today as the day you started using this technique? Notice all the times you've been able to use this technique. How much more has this helped you to make your life better?

# TAKE YOUR CUSTOMER BACK TO THE FUTURE - WORKSHEET

Can you defer payments in a 90 day trial? What about a $1 trial with the second payment in 30, 60, 90 days or payments spread out after a $1 trial? What are some options to move this as a future decision?

_____

_____

_____

Write out the question I gave you but in your words. You can copy it word-for-word to get the hang of it. Sculpt it with your vocabulary and write it so you get comfortable with this question.

"If you were to imagine what it's like 12 months from now, after deciding to start (buy, invest, etc) today, how good does it feel to know you made the right decision now?"

_____

_____

_____

What are other ways you can frame the decision as something in the future?

_____

_____

_____

Register to download printable copies of all the worksheets mentioned in this book at http://persuasiontheory.com/u/ffsm-book

# COMPARED TO WHAT?

In a past life, I was in the cemetery business. Pun intended. I sold cemetery and funerals to people still alive. It's called "pre-need" in the industry. (It's probably the only thing you can sell and truly call "pre-need." It's scary thought but you ain't getting out of this one alive.)

When I had a customer at the cemetery, I would drive him around the cemetery in a golf cart to let him get an idea of where his various options are located. As we drove around the cemetery, I would point out a *small* private mausoleum for two people he could own for only $75,000. Then I would point out a lovely private estate which allows burial for up to 8 family members. It has a private, nicely manicured garden area and they start at only $30,000. (This is a much better option based on a per-person cost but the mausoleum is truly more beautiful, in my opinion.)

If you're like most of my customers you're probably thinking, "Holy crap that's a lot of money to die! I would never spend $30,000 to be buried. Just throw me out in a pine box." (A pine box, aka a casket, is over $1000, if that really is your desire.)

Now, part of the reason I did this was to test and see if

the bigger sale was something that actually might interest them. I try to appeal to vanity for those that want it. What I didn't understand at the time was, I was giving them a price point (a comparison point) to relate what the cost of a cemetery space is now. And when we start discussing their plans the price of $1000 for a plot wouldn't seem as expensive.

Most people who come to a cemetery have no idea what costs are involved. A funeral, cremation, or a burial all have various options and details to work out. Now, with a $75,000 and a $30,000 comparison point, the $1000 plot isn't *as* shocking.

**Remember this: No decision is made in a vacuum.**

No matter what you buy **you are always referencing that decision against something.**

If you sell how to get rich quick schemes, your customer is weighing his options against his future income potential and what he makes now. If you sell an eBook, you're compared against traditional books and other media. If you sell seminars, you compare against other media for learning. If you sell investments, you're compared against interest rates, perceived safety, and future values.

You're also comparing against money spent to put food on the table, rent, and a new TV. And the random ideas people have jammed into their head watching infomercials, or from chatter around the water cooler at work, are also battling their way through your customer's brain.

Wow. You're up against a lot!

Is this helping you realize the importance of setting a

large comparison point?

In my insurance agency, our marketing emphasized the fact we could shop eight different insurance companies with one phone call or by filling out our easy online quote form. Most people are familiar with traditional insurance company marketing. The insurance company wants you to call them for **one** insurance quote from only that company.

Our marketing changed the comparison. I explained how you could spend at least two hours calling eight different insurance companies or you could call us for only 17 minutes, and we'll quote eight insurance companies for you. We could save you time *and* money. We were able to change it from merely a money decision to a time and money decision.

So give your customer his reference point for comparison. Even if it's an "apple to orange" comparison, give it. It's important for *you* set the comparison points so your customer isn't guessing and using his incorrect reference points.

Here are three ideas to anchor a comparison point:

1. Large pay-in-full price vs. small monthly payments. It's always easy to fall back on small payments if he can't pay in full.

2. Once you have the purchase, offer a less expensive upsell. If they buy a shirt for $100 then a $20 tie to upsell doesn't seem like as big of an expense and it's easier to sell.

3. You can discuss the thousands of dollars to fix a problem when someone has bought an

inferior product, or a competitor's product. When your product, priced less than the repair fees, is small in comparison.

Naturally, there are many more things you can come up with. And you can do that now...

# COMPARED TO WHAT? - WORKSHEET

What's a large number you can use to create an anchor point? It doesn't have to relate directly to what you're selling but it has to be something someone can grasp. Using the US National Debt as a point of comparison isn't helpful but the price of a new car at $50,000 is easy to comprehend. So is someone's annual salary. What things can you use in your presentation, sales letter, to relate back on against your price?

_____

_____

_____

What upsell(s) can you add to your sales process?

_____

_____

_____

Register to download printable copies of all the worksheets mentioned in this book at http://persuasiontheory.com/u/ffsm-book

# DISTRACT AND SWITCH

Have you ever felt confused and overwhelmed when buying something? Not necessarily an information overload type of confusion, the type of confusion where you feel like your questions haven't been answered. As you go through the process the salesperson comes up with elegant answers that dance around the question and confuse you a little more. Yet, after everything, you still bought the product.

We've all been through it. Again, I think of the car buying experience. There are many details you want to work out and the salespeople do the little, "let me go ask my manager," routine. You end up forgetting many of the things going on and just want it to end. So you finally give in and buy.

Generally, distraction is a technique you would use when there are problems with the product or service. They may not be huge problems but little flaws that may not make the customer happy. (Like the details in the car finance agreement?)

Instead of fixing the flaws, or addressing them and the resistance around the issue, it's easier to distract away from the problems by pointing out other advantages or creating confusion around the flawed pieces.

This really isn't a great technique and I don't encourage it. It's only best for your own personal entertainment when you want to confuse friends or family. Just go off on things that don't matter. My bride hates it when I do this but it's still fun (for me).

Work on fixing your product. Or, acknowledge the issue and make them Resist the Resistance (in the section, Working with Reactance). This is a better way of working with it and will make your customer happier, reduce refunds, and make your life a lot easier.

# DISTRACT AND SWITCH - WORKSHEET

Identify the problems with your product or service.

Where is it hard for the customer to use?

Where doesn't it work?

How can you fix these?

_____

_____

_____

Register to download printable copies of all the worksheets mentioned in this book at http://persuasiontheory.com/u/ffsm-book

# WORKING WITH THE SKEPTIC - SUMMARY

Here's a quick summary of the techniques for working with the Skeptic.

- I Guarantee It!
- The Art Of The Reframe
- Take Your Customer Back To The Future
- Compared To What?
- Distract And Switch

# SECTION 3:
# WORKING WITH THE LUMP (INERTIA)

According to Wikipedia: "Inertia is the resistance of any physical object to a change in its state of motion or rest, or the tendency of an object to resist any change in its motion."

Inertia is your biggest challenge.

However, you need to recognize **inertia isn't about you, your offer, or your sales process.**

**Inertia is inside your buyer and grows from his life experience.**

It can be his past failures and disappointments replaying over and over in his mind.

It can be his belief he already owns or knows what you're selling.

It can be his fear of looking foolish to his friends, or you.

It can be his anxiety about how it will affect other areas in his life.

Whatever is going on inside the mind of your customer is what's stopping him from considering *any* decision.

Inertia sometimes appears before you have the opportunity to present your benefits. If he won't consider your offer, it doesn't matter what benefits you present anyhow. Does it?

Other times, he reads your sales letter, or listens to your offer, yet he won't commit. Something from the past, something inside, keeps him from moving forward.

Inertia is your biggest challenge because you have to figure it out. If you can't, you won't ever have the opportunity to do your little sales dance.

# INERTIA OVERVIEW- WORKSHEET

Think about the times you've struggled with people who weren't interested or just "tuned you out." What was unique about them? Were there any common patterns you can observe now?

_____

_____

_____

What are items in your product or service that would cause someone to feel insecure or less confident? Where is it difficult to use or understand?

_____

_____

_____

Register to download printable copies of all the worksheets mentioned in this book at http://persuasiontheory.com/u/ffsm-book

# BOOST YOUR CUSTOMER'S SELF-ESTEEM

You're obviously an intelligent person or you wouldn't be reading this. You definitely wouldn't have read this far. Most people give up and let life take them from one situation to the next. Those people never fully consider the ways you can influence an outcome. You should be proud of yourself for realizing you have control over so many areas of your life. And you should be proud you're making these moments even better.

How do you feel about that?

I am sincere. I mean what I wrote. I deeply believe you're an intelligent person. Anyone searching to improve their life and learn more about how people behave is intelligent. You *should* be proud of yourself, if you weren't.

If you felt some pride, were you feeling pride before you read that? Did any more pride grow after reading that? (I hope)

In reality, we all have our fears and our failures haunting us from the past. They lay there in your unconscious, like still water growing stinky, black mold.

The scent arises as a warning to keep you from making the same mistakes again and again.

Do you remember that time a teacher said you probably won't amount to much? Or, maybe a parent said you were destined to achieve great things and you don't feel like you've done that yet? Maybe you wanted to start a business and haven't? Or you've had a business fail? Maybe you didn't get that job or promotion you wanted because you screwed up somewhere? Maybe you bought something that didn't live up to its hype (more than once)?

I'm sure you can find many areas you've failed in the past (if you want to feel bad for a while). I'd rather hit my thumb with a hammer than dwell on any failures I've lived through in my life.

I don't want you to feel bad. We all have baggage. It's part of life and part of learning. (Put any negative feelings aside now and feel proud again! Remember, you're smart.)

Your customer is not looking back at his past failures as examples where he can change and grow. Instead, "there's this feeling." There's a feeling sitting in the pit of his stomach. It's a pain that grows whenever someone reminds him of taking a step forward. There's no conscious reason for it, but it stops him dead.

This is inertia. It's a protective reaction everyone has, and you have to build confidence in your customer so he will feel strong enough to buy.

The goal is to give the customer a sense of pride, confidence, and success for his past.

Have you ever been around someone that makes you feel better than you think you are? When you begin discussing your inabilities, this person has a magical power that transforms everything about you. There aren't many people out there like this, and when you've met someone like this you remember him.

Be that person.

You want to give your customer the confidence he needs to use what you're selling. You don't need to lie to him. There's success in everyone. You have to find it and pull it out.

When discussing retirement planning with customers, I would determine the amount he needed at retirement so he could live comfortably. It's always a gigantic sum of money. The amount will overwhelm anyone who isn't already financially set.

One way I could ease the fears is to show the success he achieved by managing his finances up to today. It could be as simple as pointing out he saved $500 over the last year (a big feat for many of people). Then, after building on the small successes, we can start moving to the next decisions.

In a sales letter it's a little different. You don't know each person's challenge or success. You have to make assumptions.

If you're selling to beginners, make sure your product is easy enough for a beginner to use. In your sales copy, demonstrate the simplicity and compare it to things they've most likely accomplished without frustration.

If you're selling to an advanced market, you want to give examples an experienced user can relate with, and has completed successfully. With an advanced market it is okay for your copy to say your product isn't for the beginner. By excluding beginners, you're giving those past the newbie stage a bit of pride; they're part of a special group. They've passed the 'beginner' stage and qualify for this next step, boosting their confidence.

Hopefully, when you read the beginning of this section you felt a little better about yourself. I complimented you as an intelligent person and told you how you were better than the average. This too is an example of building confidence. Yes, it was a little cheesy but I want to be obvious so you have an example to work from.

Now, as you continue feeling better about yourself, go through the worksheet. It's okay to stop occasionally and reflect on how this will help you. That's what intelligent people do anyhow.

# BOOST YOUR CUSTOMER'S SELF-ESTEEM - WORKSHEET

We discussed "free trials" before. Do you have the ability to offer a free trial to allow your customer to feel comfortable (confident) they can use it?

_____

_____

_____

What are things in your customer's lives you can relate with what you're selling? What are similar products or services they've made decisions about and used successfully?

_____

_____

_____

How can you reframe their past "mistakes" as the reason they're smarter and can make an educated decision today, now that they've "learned" from that mistake?

_____

_____

_____

Register to download printable copies of all the worksheets mentioned in this book at http://persuasiontheory.com/u/ffsm-book

# BRING IT DOWN TO SIZE - INERTIA

You want to make sure your customer can easily accomplish whatever it is your offering. Making your request seem small makes it easy for your buyer to take those first steps.

This works really well when you also Boost Your Customer's Confidence (the previous technique).

Bring It Down To Size was explained in detail on dealing with Reactance. Go read that section for specific examples on how to minimize a request again.

# BRING IT DOWN TO SIZE - WORKSHEET INERTIA

Identify all the steps in your sales process when you require a commitment, or some sort of action, for your customer to take. They can be the sale, making an appointment to meet with them, fill out a form, whatever. List them here:

_____

_____

_____

Take each step and brainstorm ways you can make the request seem smaller. How can you make it seem easier?

_____

_____

_____

Register to download printable copies of all the worksheets mentioned in this book at http://persuasiontheory.com/u/ffsm-book

# MAKE THEM RESIST THEIR INERTIA

This was also discussed in part 2 on dealing with Reactance (Make Them Resist Their Resistance).

I know you may not want to go back to reread it now but reading the examples there will give you very unique understanding of the lesson.

Yes! I just used the technique Acknowledge Inertia in that paragraph (I'm so sneaky). By writing, "I know you may not want to…" I've acknowledged the resistance you may have had. Again, Inertia is something from your buyer's history that stops them. When you acknowledge it, it's like loosening the lid on a jar. The jar is still not open but, now that it's loose, it's a lot easier to remove the lid and open it completely.

# ACKNOWLEDGE THE INERTIA - WORKSHEET

Where are the points of friction in your sales process?

_____

_____

_____

    Where would it be worthwhile to test resisting the resistance?

"I know you may not want to but (your desired action)."
Or,
"I know you may not fully agree with this but (what you want them to agree on)."

_____

_____

_____

    Register to download printable copies of all the worksheets mentioned in this book at http://persuasiontheory.com/u/ffsm-book

# WEAR THEM DOWN

Constant repetition. E-mail follow up. Repeat mail offers. Eventually, curiosity will build up and he will inquire.

In traditional face-to-face sales, I don't encourage using this technique. Your customer will feel like you've mentally beat him up until he buys. Go back again to the car dealership experience and you can relate to this technique. They wear you out with constant trips to the manager. They need to see if management can meet your price, get approval for financing, check if the car you want is actually on the lot, etc. It's not a pleasant experience (I think I've picked on them enough in this workbook).

Don't do this to your customers unless you want them to feel bad about your experience together.

In marketing, this technique is a bit different. When you have someone on your email or mailing list, repetition increases the chance your customer will buy.

Online, you can email your offer in various ways every day. Naturally you want to make sure you're providing value beyond a sales pitch. If you fail to give any value, you'll only end up with a high unsubscribe rate (or worse, marked as spam).

However, email marketing is practically free for you to increase the *mental impressions* you make. Have you ever received multiple emails and eventually something inside you said, "Alright, what's this all about?" You decide click to read more about the product? That's this process at work. This repetition increases your curiosity and desire. (I have an article on my site in with a link in the resource section on email marketing)

It's similar in direct mail. A few years ago, in my old insurance agency, we rolled over $1.6 million into retirement accounts in 12 months directly from our monthly newsletter. We never directly mentioned investments but routinely discussed taxes, retirement planning, and IRAs in general. After a few months, we started receiving calls from people wondering what to do with their old 401k or IRA. These turned into appointments and into a dozen sales. The repetition in the newsletter did the selling and generated the interest.

Marketing caveat: If someone asks you to take them off your list you should remove them immediately. Your email system should include a 1-click unsubscribe option to comply with spam laws.

With that said, as long as someone is willing to read your offer you have the ability to influence him and can take advantage of it.

Mail often and make sure you're providing value and curiosity to get your customer off his sloth-like ass.

I have a list of recommended email marketing solutions you can check out at: http://persuasiontheory.com/u/ffsm-book

# WEAR THEM DOWN - WORKSHEET

Create a monthly marketing calendar so you can plan your annual marketing strategy for various products.

_____

_____

_____

If you have an email list, are you sending emails at least once per week with information that relates to what you sell?

_____

_____

_____

Do you send monthly newsletters where you can offer products for new and existing customers? Do you have an email list? What ways can you start implementing a strategy to keep your product/services on the mind of your customers?

_____

_____

_____

Register to download printable copies of all the worksheets mentioned in this book at http://persuasiontheory.com/u/ffsm-book

# CREATE DISRUPTIONS

You're in a trance…most of the day. Almost every moment of every day you're in some form of trance. Your unconscious automatically runs the show. Your conscious mind is distracted with little things and your unconscious keeps you alive, safe, and functioning.

Your customer is in a trance too. His unconscious is working hard to keep him protected and safe. It runs the same routines day in and day out. This trance is behind the resistance called inertia.

## Snap your buyer out of his trance.

As they say in traditional sales and marketing, "You have to get the customer's attention." This will help you do that and make more sales in the process.

In research[5], students went door-to-door selling note cards for charity. In the some households they said, "a packet of 8 cards is **three dollars; it's a bargain!**" This

---

[5] Davis, B., & Knowles, E. S. (1999). A Disrupt-Then-Reframe Technique of Social Influence. Journal of Personality & Social Psychology, 76(2), 192-199

approach sold 35% of the households. Other households were told "a packet of 8 cards is **300 pennies; it's a bargain!**" This disruption, the change from "three dollars" to "300 pennies," almost doubled sales to 65%.

They also tried other versions of the phrase with "it's a bargain at 300 pennies" and simply "they're 300 pennies." These only sold in the 30% to 35% range, the same as the control phrase, "three dollars; it's a bargain!"

When the students disrupted the customer's thought with "300 pennies," it allowed the sales message "it's a bargain!" to bypass the resistance. It creates a brief state of confusion allowing the message to be accepted. (If you're familiar with Milton Erickson, and his use of confusion in hypnosis, this will sound familiar. If not, that's okay too.)

In a similar study[6], college students sold cupcakes at the school for 50 cents. Randomly they said, "I'm selling this **half-cake** for 50 cents; it's delicious!" or "I'm selling this **cupcake** for 50 cents; it's delicious!" The change in sales results was the same as the 300 pennies research with "half-cake" outselling by almost double. Because "half-cake" is not a common way to say cupcake it interrupts thought and allowed the message "it's delicious" to slide by the inertia.

## How Much Fun Will You Have With This Technique?

My bride always laughs at me when I do this but I love it. Plus, it's a great way for you to practice watching interrupts work.

---

[6] Knowles, E.A., & Linn, J.A. (2004). *Resistance and Persuasion*. New Jersey: Lawrence Erlbaum Associates, Inc.

Wherever I go, I ask whoever is helping us, "How much fun are you having today?" instead of "How are you?" I've asked this question to thousands of people over the last 10 years and I love how it opens people up.

It's an obvious interruption. Think about it, when was the last time anyone asked you, "How much fun are you having today?" You usually get the routine "How are you?" and reply with a mindless, "not bad and you?" Neither of you remember this piece of your conversation, if you want to call it a conversation.

The elegance of the question, "How much fun are you having today?" assumes you're already having some fun today and asks you to recognize how much of it you've actually experienced.

Don't get me wrong, this isn't a panacea to make people excited about life. Most people often reply, "None, I'm at work." But they'll smile or chuckle when they say it.

After their reply, I've altered their perception. If they said "none," I can now say something as simple as, "That's too bad. I promise you'll start having fun now that I've been here." (With a grin) They may give a goofy reply. It doesn't matter. I get to practice working with resistance and I get to make someone's day a little better. And, I have a little fun myself.

I started asking this because I noticed most people don't recognize the fun in life. It only takes a little attention to enjoy things more.

Give this a try the next time you're at a grocery store, restaurant, bank, on the phone, wherever. Ask the checkout clerk or the waitress, "How much fun are you having today?" (Emphasize "you" in the question and remember the word "today" to give them a time frame to process the question. Also, make it sound playful.) Notice how they react.

Let me know through my contact page (http://persuasiontheory.com/contact/) or via email (Fox@PersuasionTheory.com) what you experience. If you run across any challenging replies I'd love to help you out.

## How To Use Disrupt And Reframe In Writing

The first step in copywriting is to get attention. This is why your headline is so critical. You want to grab your reader by the eyeballs and make him want to keep reading.

Here are a few classic headlines using a Disrupt and Reframe technique as an example:

- "Amazing Secret Discovered By One-Legged Golfer Adds 50 Yards To Your Drives, Eliminates Hooks And Slices…And Can Slash Up To 10 Strokes From Your Game Almost Overnight!" – John Carlton
- How I Made A Fortune With A "Fool" Idea
- At 60 Miles Per Hour The Loudest Noise In This New Rolls Royce Comes From The Electric Clock – David Ogilvy

Notice how these headlines take a basic idea and make you think, "This is so outrageous, how?"

How could a one-legged golfer help me improve my golf game? How can a foolish idea make someone a fortune? How can an electric clock be the loudest thing in a car at 60 miles per hour?

What these examples do is create a slight state of confusion in your mind, which briefly jolts you out of your trance. Then, while you're in this brief state of confusion, you pay attention and the suggestion (your product or service benefit) is allowed to drop in and arouse curiosity.

It's that simple.

# CREATE DISRUPTIONS - WORKSHEET

What are clever ways you can restate what you're selling so it's a disruption? Think beyond price (300 pennies) too.

_____

_____

_____

Construct a list of words you can weave into a conversation that may induce brief states of confusion. These also can be little metaphors or odd sayings you don't commonly hear ('grab them by the eyeballs'). Sprinkle them into your message when you need to get a point across.

_____

_____

_____

Register to download printable copies of all the worksheets mentioned in this book at http://persuasiontheory.com/u/ffsm-book

# THE ALTERNATE CHOICE

Imagine you made a search on Google and clicked a link to arrive at a website. On the website was a brief description about what you want. Then it reads, "To better help you please choose one of two options:

- Click here if you are male
- Click here if you are female

When you arrive at a website, you're searching for something specific. As good as Google is at finding the right website, you're never sure if you'll get what you expect. When you're presented with an option like this, you're more likely to click an option…and actually read the page after you click.

Remember, **with inertia, you're stuck.** You're not moving in any direction. One of the ways to get you engaged and moving (in any direction) is to give you a choice. It gets you focused on answering the question and moving out of the stuck state. It brings you into the sales process and starts you moving.

## Choice In Payment Options

One place I've fallen for this is on a sales letter for a

product I might want to own but I don't want to buy. It's usually a product where I already own something similar. However, I read the sales letter anyhow because I'm curious what they're offering. When I get to the "Buy Now" button there are a couple of payment options. I can pay in full for $100. I can pay with two payments for $50 or with 3 payments of $35 each (these are examples, obviously).

When this happens, I start thinking to myself, "well, I can make three $35 payments easily without it pissing anyone off at home (my bride)…" This decision took me from my stoic position ("I already own something like this. I don't need it.") to choosing which payment option is best for my situation today ("I can afford to get this. I wonder what I'm missing."). I'm sucked back into the buying process.

## An Object In Motion…

Once you've made a choice, you're engaged again. If you remember Newton's Laws of Motion, an object in motion (or rest) remains in motion (at rest) unless acted on by an outside force. Your job is to give a choice to take them from their resting position and get them moving in your direction.

In the example above, where you choose "male" or "female" on a website, you're getting your customer to make small commitments. Once he makes the initial decision, he's more likely to read the page. One commitment leads to another.

Start with small decisions to get him started moving, then increase his involvement. The point is simply to get him into the process so he begins moving. Once you have motion you can begin to control the direction with your benefits.

# ALTERNATE CHOICE - WORKSHEET

What are areas you run into Inertia?

_____

_____

_____

What questions can you ask that move the customer towards a decision to move forward?

_____

_____

_____

Register to download printable copies of all the worksheets mentioned in this book at http://persuasiontheory.com/u/ffsm-book

# WORKING WITH THE LUMP (INERTIA) - SUMMARY

Here's a quick summary of the techniques for working with Inertia.

- Boost Your Customer's Self-Esteem
- Bring It Down To Size - Inertia
- Make Them Resist Their Inertia
- Wear Them Down
- Create Disruptions
- The Alternate Choice

# WHAT WILL YOU DO NOW?

You've now loaded your toolbox with new tools for your persuasive artistry. There are hundreds of ways you can apply these techniques; far beyond the examples I gave. Push them to the limits. Please, let me know what you've tested and your results.

Also, I really hope this gives you additional ways to think about your persuasion skills. Understanding resistance and the internal friction your customer experiences will make everything you do a lot easier and open more doors. You may not think in specific techniques but you've become more effective simply because of this new awareness. That's okay. Enjoy it.

Let me know how I can help you. Where do you struggle and what stops you in all areas of persuasion, marketing, sales, business?

Now go and register to *download the worksheets* and the *bonus material*:

http://persuasiontheory.com/u/ffsm-book

Have fun!

**Now put your new influence skills to work and persuade your friends to buy a copy of this book.**

## TO CONTACT THE AUTHOR:

Matt Fox
PersuasionTheory.com
Find Me On Twitter - @PersuasionFox
And Google+ - http://persuasiontheory.com/u/p

www.ingramcontent.com/pod-product-compliance
Lightning Source LLC
Chambersburg PA
CBHW051216170526
45166CB00005B/1929